Haunts

Laura Cherry

Cooper
Dillon

Copyright © 2010 by Laura Cherry
First edition

Cooper Dillon Books
San Diego, California
CooperDillon.com

Cover Art: "4700 Adams" by Daniel Thedell
Cover Design: Max Xiantu

ISBN-10: 0-9841928-3-2
ISBN-13: 978-0-9841928-3-0

Printed in the United States

Acknowledgments:

These poems have been published in the following journals and anthologies:

Agenda Broadsheet 5: Ice-Encrusted Firefighter Cradles a Cup of
    Coffee

Argestes: Testing the Waters

Asphodel: Haunted

Bark: The Whippet Catches Worms

Flyway: On the Bridge

Forklift, Ohio: My Therapist Lets Down Her Hair, I Demand an
    Explanation

H_NGM_N: Layoffs, Glimpse, We Could Use a Few More
    Members at the Thousand-Dollar Level

LA Review: Hating Poetry

Lettters to the World (Red Hen Press): The Nurse and the Principal

Literary Mama: Dishes, Lila: Found Poem

Poem, Revised (Marion Street Press): Jack in Love

Present Tense: Writing and Art by Young Women (Calyx Press): On
    the Bridge

Reed Magazine. Laughing, Whispering, Weeping

The Vocabula Review: Story for a Dull World, The Light through the Rain, Settlement, Cab Ride to Logan, After Li Ch'ing Chao, The Nurse and the Principal, Restaurant, Burning the Shed

Vocabula Bound: Outbursts, Insights, Explanations and Oddities, ed. Robert Hartwell Fiske (Marion Street Press): Settlement, Cab Ride to Logan

The following poems appeared in the chapbook *What We Planted*, winner of the 2002 Philbrick Poetry Award by the Providence Athenaeum: After Li Ch'ing Chao, Dishes, Neighbors, Haunted, The Husk, Trying, Indolence, Autumn, Nightingale, Melancholy, The Nurse and the Principal, Crabs, Virgins, Sniffing You Out, Chapter Book, Flying Dreams, Sleep, Visit

Laura Cherry would like to thank her family, especially Ted German, Lila Cherry-German, Virginia Cherry, and Elaine German; wise counselors Stuart Dischell, Steve Orlen, Dan Tobin, and Brooks Haxton; excellent readers Timothy Gager, Laurie Junkins, Norman Waskler, and the Robins (Diane Gilliam, Jannett Highfill, and constant darling Leslie Shinn); the Munson-Palombas, for inspiration for a number of these poems; dear friends Erica Burditt, Seana Shiffrin, and Liz Hirsch; Adam, Max, Colleen, Daniel, and Taylor; and all the loved ones who fed and watered this work.

TABLE OF CONTENTS

LAUGHING, WHISPERING, WEEPING

EVERYTHING BUT YOU

SCENES I NEVER MADE

Haunts

Laura Cherry

LAUGHING, WHISPERING, WEEPING

Story for a Dull World

Those coffee-drinking monks knew what they were doing.
I can see them now in their cappuccino-colored robes,
running to morning prayers, planting rutabagas with zeal,
illuminating manuscripts in flagrant teal and wild vermilion.

Those monks had pizzazz. Their eighteen-hour days
passed in the wink of a dilated pupil. They were supermonks,
their devotion unprecedented, their energy infinite,
their coffee plantations fingering the horizon.

One year the crop failed. Leaves slowly browned,
turned papery as tobacco. When the last plant was lost
the monks mourned, chanting feverishly. A few
martyred themselves. Then the headaches struck. None survived.

Ice-Encrusted Firefighter Cradles a Cup of Coffee

photo caption, Boston Globe

Somewhere across unimaginable distance, birds
call, a low repeating note; bodies unlock
in the slow light, desire unwinding loop by loop
like a spool of ribbon; evening catches
the release of jasmine. Here the wall of fire
slams into the ceiling of cold, building
the infernal house we work all night to wreck.
Like miners we chip away, like miners we are blackened
inside and out. For days we will spit soot.
We swim in a sea of Gore-Tex and sweat
that will freeze us if we stop. Twenty below,
then ten; at last there is a sun, so that we know
we are not underground, just in the shambles
of a mechanical passion, our nameless fear hardening
the way snow turns to rain and then to ice.
Love doesn't enter it by a long shot.
It is trouble to love our families after this.
In the white sunrise someone brings me
this godforsaken cup of coffee, the AP photographer
steps out of his car for a few fast frames.
The air melts and runs like glass.

I look up and split my face open at the mouth.

Cab Ride to Logan

Hours before I'm usually awake, I'm ready:
coffeed up, lipsticked and hairsprayed, corporate
face on, posture undaunted by the laptop slung
over my shoulder. The driver's not much for conversation.
I could go for some, to fend off sleep, but nothing
gets past my throat, primed for meeting-speak. So I sit
in princessy silence, hands folded neatly in my lap.
Sun flashes on storefronts like an old, old promise:
even this cold sunrise whispers now of spring.
I like the silent ride, now smooth, now struggling--
gliding through Somerville, lurching down 93,
watching the illegal lane changes in the Callahan Tunnel.
I am clearly, irreparably urban. I suppose it's too late
for me and the natural world. Still, as the taxi noses
its expert way to Terminal C, I am given the day's
single nice surprise: a flock of small birds rising,
each one as moving, as lyrical in ascent
as a tiny, luminous plane taking off on schedule.

Settlement

Stop holding the landscape hostage. Give back
the forsythia at least, or the boats on the Charles,
or even the willows before they start to bud,
and then you can have them again. Free up
one of the shades of blue sky, one type of weather;
relinquish wet paving-stones, oil-slicked puddles,
the satisfaction of heaving open the window
to breathe. Let me have squat, hairy, grounded
bulbs; grass-nubs; snails with their tender,
sprouting horns; the smell of gas stations; first
sunlight the color of weak lemonade. Of course middles
and ends are yours, and temperature, and impact, life
in its full growth of green. All that flourishes
I'll tithe to you willingly: sweep it into the pile
of gold in your lap. But allow me beginnings, something
starting somewhere, partial rights to the memory, my dear
disappearing love, of what I thought we'd never finish.

I Demand an Explanation

Has a Maine lobster got your tongue,
or has a Charlie Chaplin film festival
silenced you for months? Surely your next move
will be a twenty-one bagpipe apology,
with you in a hot air balloon high above
reproach, flaunting your star-spangled manner.
Might you fling a thousand stuffed bears
from a skyscraper, hoping I'm in New York?
How about shooting a murky pearl at me
from a silver pistol? Mail me your mother.
Stir-fry an armadillo. Trim all the hedges
in the yard to spell my name. Hang
in my doorway in gravity boots and refuse
to move until I forgive you. I forgive you.

Testing the Waters

He wakes like fingers snapped at nine, takes
the pill that keeps the vivid, nibbling world
gray and at arm's length. This room's

the worse for his wear, its heaped ashtrays
and crusty plates outlined in the day's best light,
smoky as a torch. Curtains up, here comes the heart –

a beat late – wheezy accordion cranking out schmaltz,
toothless performer upstaged by the quick brain
at every turn: *Sink or swim, pal, swim or sink.*

His chops are shaky but his legs take the stairs
and the sidewalk makes his boot heels click
that old tune, the straight and narrow,

halleluia. No fish or sweet bread on Sunday,
but the view's open. It's not a cove, just
a short sweep of rock, then miles of rank blue

he reads like an invitation. He wants to dare
that slick surface, to spray-paint across the horizon
I WAS HERE. SUCKERS! He's a stone

that only shows its colors in sea water,
and he's stone dry. He's on the half shell, shivering.
He's on the next ship out, one leg

over the side. Drunk with air, Heart starts the show
again, but Brain steals it with a single line:
Out of cigarettes. Ears cold. He heads back

to the unlit hall, the room always showing him the door.
The shared bathroom, for God's sake. Sharpens
a pencil – *no work today. No problem-solving,*

please. Do yourself a favor. He does. Under
the music and under his breath, he'll rehearse
his getaway: breast stroke, butterfly, crawl.

On the Bridge

Late Sunday afternoon, driving east through Pennsylvania.
A hush behind the Last Exit Before Toll signs.
Love is asleep in the passenger seat, and may never

wake up again. One at a time, you unclench
your hands from the wheel; shaking them out,
you think for the first time of work, the office,

life flooding back like blood to a numb limb.
You think: those predawn mornings, too blue-black
for your dull head, Love left lying in the bed,

that ugly hour too quick for coffee. You think:
the whir of the computer and its white screen, bits
of you in its heart and brain and teeth.

There's a rush, a commotion, or else
it is only you there typing, alphabetizing, playing
mother to plastic, metal and paper. Either way,

nothing more is asked of you than blankness. Later,
it is all you ask of yourself, sipping wine, cooking
dinner, bringing two plates to the television.

Here in the cold car you blink,
you reassume your life, no less tired than it was
on Friday. Love stirs and leans toward the window.

You get the toll ready, three cool quarters in your palm.
You are on the bridge, its long and right design,
the cars spaced with perfect symmetry, one by one by one.

The Light Through the Rain

after Wallace Stevens

The trip in the rain has cost you your shoes,
sloshing through puddles and dreaming of Hartford,
watching the sky blear like noontime in Norway.

You think you smell ocean in the air; some
quality of wind, its shaking, recalls
beachy days of incessant pounding and pulse,

the tricolor sea, emerald, violet, and white,
alive in the manner of all remembering.
You used to see horses in sea-foam

or clouds. Spiral shells were souvenirs
of those days when the light shaded,
quickly and suddenly, yellow to purple

to the stage-light effect of the full moon
intoning its eminence in the wide sky.
You wonder what thing you have seen to rival

that spectacle: some moment of visible words,
floating hands, a mouth soft as twilight?
Those attitudes, fleeting poetic postures, never last.

Women do not hear enough from you.
You cannot tell them all the round smooth sleeps
they bring; they are gone before the river

of your mind can reach them. Some naked
cry in the air now drops you into the clear
wet knowledge of walking, each muscle

a heartbeat of pain, the whisk of your shoe-soles
rhythmic and worn. The ocean breeze is gone.
Ahead, an irised sun slowly breaks loose.

My therapist lets down her hair

literally, an unthinkable raven freefall
through canyons of the unknown, beauty
visited on the world by force and by consent, O
the glories of transference! It is the shadow
self made visible, made an embrace,
made dark wine in clear crystal that reveals
a landscape as it is drunk: the peaks
of mountains never before imagined, and
lakes of a thousand blue surfaces, each
a deeper sapphire than the last. See
the sweetness unleashed, unbraided, the hair
somehow unveiling, as it falls and is pushed
back, falls and is pushed back, the honest
difficult life more precious than the loveliest
delusion; see as if it were meant for you alone
the truth that will set you free.

We Could Use a Few More Members at the
Thousand-Dollar Level

Again they've left the mike on so the fitful
jangling phone is louder than the music.

How they must dread these ten endless days:
the manager toting her overnight bag to work;

volunteers drooping over their donuts; deejays
rambling, imagining our prolonged wince;

same recorded celebrity shuck, same coffee-mad
CD-dropping mania, willing to pledge back

almost anything for *your call*. But they persist
in the biennial slog with regretfully few

Jerry Lewis telethon moments. You *will* walk alone,
public radio station in the windowless basement

of a small-time college, sending out your pleas
to the profit-polluted autumn air.

Layoffs

This row of cubicles is haunted.
One by one or in bunches,
the occupants picked off, midday,
dispossessed, made to leave at once.

Now, the monitors staring and silent,
notebooks left in hopeful attitudes,
paper clips, Post-it pads in every hue:
mine, all mine!

Urban Spring

Along with the usual mid-May motes
hanging lit in allergenic air, this morning
something fiery drips from the ceiling
onto the subway steps, intermittent flashing wet

the disembarkers lurch to miss.
What is it? Not rain, not leftover rain.
No anti-antiseptic smell: not piss.
Some solvent, maybe, some resolvent

in case we hadn't yet made up our minds
to do the day, to enter the buildings
and push the hours into a pile.
We wobble up and out, a single file.

Window Hawks

I can't stop talking about the hawks,
red-tail hawks who built a nest
of stripped sticks and evergreens and mouse fur
on the ninth-floor ledge, just
inches from the fabric cubicle walls
on this side of the window, and who
take turns settling over two spotted eggs
though the web sites say it's the female's job.
She sits rapt, attentive, calm.
On his watch, he fidgets a bit.
It's the news, unfit to print:
her sparrow snacks, our fear of window washers.
Hardly speechless with praise, all day I say
red-tail hawks, red-tail hawks.

You should see the nest.

Hawks Learn to Fly

It's awkward to call them *chicks*, though they are:
just two months hatched, already full-size,

knowing-eyed, wicked of claw, hopping knock-kneed
past the window, new spotted feathers ruffling in the wind.

One flapped its way down, ungainly as a rooster,
to cling upside-down to the parking garage grate.

There are stories of rescue, misguided bystanders
carting them in bags to the rooftop again.

Hawk in the elevator! Just now one hunches immobile
on a high ledge. Somewhere its mother screams.

Laughing, Whispering, Weeping

On Fridays you get up to lie down:
in the early morning when you're
barely awake enough to get there

almost on time, what you say then
is a kind of talking in bed, isn't it –
only the two of you hear, maybe only he

remembers, caffeinated and taking notes.
But as you keep your standing date
horizontally, as you skinny-dip

in that pool of his attention, warmed
by dreams and confessions, displaying
the vermilion tattoos of failure,

as you yell at him and – unorthodox
methods – are yelled back at, that layer
of self you lose just leaves you shining,

scrubbed down and serene, ready again
for the vicious meetings and inedible lunches,
the cost-benefit analysis and power yoga.

Everyone wants to touch you on Fridays,
lit up like an office park,
wearing the world like it actually fits.

The Whippet Catches Worms

Nose of an anteater, paws of an angel,
Greta Garbo dances through the garden.
She's a metaphor unto herself,

so light she scarcely dents the mud.
What's her little past – the kennel, the trembling
car ride – next to this wet spring

when the earthworms rise to meet her
and be dangled from her snout?
It's too tender to bear,

the way she lays them carefully down
after the trot, spin and whirligig, then
seeks out the next hole, fine as a needle-poke.

Hating Poetry

Reading it under the desk
gets you a reputation at work.
Still, it won't stand up for you no matter
how you hold the book, every word meaning

two or three things, dog, god, last mouthful
of bread, but never how to dress,
get bloodstains out of carpet, punish a child,
debone a fish – the lines broken so cleverly,

each with its little bent knee,
the careful forms like jewelry boxes
that need to have their locks picked,
the wasted stick figures with their ribbons flying.

It can't keep you warm in the wind,
apologize to your best friend,
get your car from the shop,
massage even one of your toes.

If you fall down it steps over you.
If you stay down it never looks back.

Maybe I'll Stop Here

Because I only have so many fingers,
and each one lost costs me a little
more blood. Because nothing is gained
except pocket room, and a greater respect
for the genius of knives. Because
I have just enough left to work with, enough
to hail a cab without causing a scene.
Because I remember the ones I used to have,
the full complement of ten, and all they could do,
and make, and know. Because the wagging
tongues of empty glove fingers reproach me
all winter. Because there is less to love and less love
to lose. Because the memory of pain
cannot satisfy the longings of those small ghosts
demanding retribution, calling for my head.

EVERYTHING BUT YOU

After Li Ch'ing Chao

Spring's turbulence is over,
and summer's solitude.
The house is peaceful again.
September loves the blue sky,
which loves it back.
I have let the cat into the yard
while I drink coffee on the steps.
She gets braver and braver,
staring down squirrels and small birds
with her eyes the color of grass.
The forsythia are tall as teenagers.
I have reassembled my happiness
like a cracked plate,
but not yet glued it
into its former shape.

Dishes

A thumb-smear on the tile floor, the smell
of blood, menstrual, in the room where I am
on my haunches, waiting to catch my friend
if she pitches forward, giving up what she said

she expected to: she knew it wouldn't take,
didn't even tell us until the midnight call
that fetched my sweetheart – still wearing his coat, ready
for a hospital run – and me, wielding towels.

Her husband tends the three-year-old, hectic
in the late commotion, the grownups gathered
for what must be a party, but too patient
and too sad. And when she settles on the couch –

stanched, hand on the phone – we watch the boy
rocket through the room, firm and loud in his skin,
while his father leaves to stand at the sink
and wash dishes, dishes, every dish in reach.

Neighbors

for Ann and Tony

In her sheared-off nylon coat, the woman
with white hair stands outside,
swaying and backing up slowly.
When I look again, she's gone.

We send engagement flowers
and hospital flowers. We dig
circles in the grass for lilac bushes.

Behind the brick house next to us:
an indoor pool, enormous, used only
by invisible swimmers.
All winter the windows steam and clear.

The ambulance stops down the block
and takes away the covered stretcher.
Next week, the For Sale sign goes up.

Wood fences weather in the sun.
Yelling, ten-year-olds coast the hill.
The morning glories open and close,
watching neither kindly nor unkindly.

Haunted

I knew I should have appeased the place
while it was empty: shaken salt into the corners,
swung a bell, rattled a seedy gourd,
set bowls of water in moonlight to mist the air.
I should have made a sweet vortex of smoke.

I could at least have smudged the rooms with sage.
Who knows what spirits I left untouched, vibrations
of failed marriages, shards of lonely singlehood,
the molting parrot's shriek left behind
along with droppings and talon-ripped wallpaper.

This kitchen and its faux marble surfaces
can never have inspired a meal of love.
The cabinets keep the chaos of unpacking,
commingling corn meal, cinnamon, peppermint tea.
I carry the unsatisfied place around:

sandy beaches are like slightly gritty pine floors;
even restaurants refuse to hide my own
splintery table under white linen. All weekend away,
the trees have lost leaves to the bright sky as we roamed
the sites of the season. But the rooms we left

call with familiar voices, like the lonely, living cat
who paces, deciding how to wait or get revenge.
The ancient boiler bangs pipes in our dreams.
Dogwood, maple, chrysanthemum, marigold:
what we planted pulls us back to watch the change.

Burning the Shed

for Robert

Firstly rend the disreputable boards
with a claw hammer till your arms and back
are a tree of pain. Pull and save
the nails to no purpose. Pile the splintering
paint-flecked wood in a bare patch of yard.
Even if your bonfire permit will soon expire,
even if it expires today, avoid haste.
Do not fling the match while pouring gas
or the flame will follow it to find your hands.

Afterward, haul and fit stones to form
a floor, a foundation of sorts. When
the new shed arrives, follow directions;
accept no help. Finished, it is twice as sound
as what you watched burn to ash. It looks the same.
It's small, quite small. You stain it gray.

The News from Downstairs

The neighbors are not moving.
Three times they approached the brink –
offers given and received,
children parceled out to bedrooms –
and three times stepped back,
vertiginous and reeling.

They're too much for their space,
rabbiting around in winter, gnawing
at the exits, shuddering
at our overhead thumps, crammed,
cemented into smallness.
But the neighbors are staying, friends

who bought this place with us,
and with us mourned its beige siding,
stirred compost, tended trees,
sanded the sandbox, swung the swing.
When their baby came, we walked her to sleep.
When ours came, they mowed the lawn all summer.

The neighbors are tossing it in, sticking it out,
sucking it up, trying to forget
an Eden beyond our angels tantruming
under the maple, grass clippings in their hair,
inches from the poison ivy
we keep meaning to uproot.

Lila

1. Trying

Little knot-
person, squeamish dream,
tiny vine, you are the one
we court in fear –
fingernail moon
or splinter of cells
tucked in tight.
To make this
home for you we forfeit
whatever measures most:
wine, chocolate, love,
a quiet turn of mind.
Feel welcome and frayed
as we are, counting days
or degrees,
taking aim at time,
that ricochet bulls-eye.

2. Lila

Greek for the lily.
Arabic for night.
Diminutive of Delilah,
my care won't bring us luck,

my luck won't bring us peace.
You're the string around my finger:
remember, remember this.
It comes at nineteen weeks,

just before the bombs:
your little drum protest
with its audience of one.
I hold my plans unclenched,

admire the lizard of your spine,
the wagging tongue of your heart,
your starfish hand in the picture
my finest hope to date.

3. First Sight

Transparent, amphibian,
dancing to beat the band,
you there in black and white
must be where all the juice is going,
the renegade drain on the sap that once
kept me awake till nightfall at least.
It's for you now, my eat and sleep, my water
and sun. Too little to mind, you dabble in me,
pratfall, somersault and porpoise-dive
while I watch your flutter of heart
with the tired amazement I expect
to have years to perfect.

4. Windows

The lead in these leaky antique windows,
their lovely small panes and flaking frames,
they say is bad for you, whoever you are,
thumping your wakeful hours along my skin.

So we'll roll the rugs and shroud the shelves,
pack what's precious away from dust,
and I'll go into hiding from my house
while others do the dirty work they're paid for:

push our elegant windows onto the lawn
to fit in the cheap glass and plastic wood.
For you who strain towards the world
yet scuttle from the hand or heartbeat-finder,

fickle symptom, intermittent companion,
we take a trial run at inconvenience,
put ourselves out in the cold, begin to
replace the known with the new.

5. When

So pregnant it felt professional,
still clearing closets, readying a corner
like a rabbit or cat, but numb as a tree,

dumb as a dictionary. Foolish as time,
then out of time.
A single-take scene, wavery frame

and silvery light. Three rowboats on the wall.
A few repeated phrases containing numbers.
Pretending it's not all depending on this.

6. Eighty-Four Days

Turning in my bed I hear her shift.
Eyes open wide in the dark
and the calling starts: a huff, a cluck,

a long in-breath and then the wail,
an operatic *whoop-whoop-whoop*.
I've slept four hours, or two, or almost one.

Fifteen watts light up the room
as I collect her thrashing self.
In her boat she's lone, bereft,

big enough to whack its sides;
at the breast she's lidded but intent,
determined to survive this night

of ordinary, ungodly pangs.
Cradle cap, diaper rash, baby acne, thrush,
yet still *the most beautiful*.

Folded in on me she sleeps;
drooping over her I doze
until the mockingbird starts up

his car-alarm song sequence
announcing the gritty gray-pink sky,
waking her to start the morning shift.

7. Lila: Found Poem

Lila is born
Lila is designed to be as simple as possible to use
Lila is generally shepherded by an executive board of four people
Lila is the first to admit she surrounds herself with great advisors
Lila is autobiographical? this is always hard to tell
Lila is so cool she sure wasn't a fool so glad she decided to stay in
        school Lila is so cool
Lila is a rich ceremony of song
Lila is a very suitable name
Lila is flowing in all ten directions in hundreds of streams as if from
        a fountain
Lila is considered by many to be the greatest story ever told
Lila is highly interactive
Lila is loosely based on my mother's handwriting
Lila is true poetry in motion
Lila is about to dispatch a fourth victim when a pair of police
        detectives arrives on the scene
Lila is a reasonable heroine
Lila is like visiting an old friend
Lila is the chief feature of this area
Lila is inspired by earthy trance grooves from a variety of cultures
Lila is a novel
Lila is a valuable asset to our company
Lila is new to standup but equally as addicted to the high it
        provides
Lila is facilitated best in human society
Lila is a girl

Virus

This much I know: a coughing child won't sleep.
The child who coughs could yell for me
at any time. If my rest will be similarly
wracked, why sleep? A sleeping child has deep,
exemplary breaths, melodious, face up in bed
for safety's sake. It isn't fear but dread
that keeps me up: I'll have to rise and shine
the hall light in, bring water, medicine,
convincing sympathy. At least I'm here, supine,
neither tending now nor needed to tend.
This I know: one piss-poor night follows another
nursery coughing spree. I'd rather sleep than mother.

Indolence

O, for an age so sheltered from annoy,
  That I may never know how change the moons,
    Or hear the voice of busy common sense!
                    — John Keats, "Ode to Indolence"

Clock-watching, caffeinated from white sunrise to midnight,
no time for looking at shadows and what's in them
or imagining dramas of the people on the bus, itinerary stapled
to my coat and book glued to my hand, I commute.
March is a pear so green it feels frozen to the bite.
Winter's cough lingers, a fishy gluten in the throat.
In parking lots dirty snow piles melt to feed
the flowers, but here even love can't compensate
for the laundry undone, the thoughts that won't slow for sleep.
The tracery on my eyelids reminds me of what's left
on the checklist, the dancing figures on the page,
the line at Starbucks reaching almost to the door,
track lights staring down opalescent and comfortless as stars.

Autumn

She brought, mainly, misery and regret:
at first a baby bird gasping to be fed,
then tearing out your liver every night
for the crime of having discovered her.
By day in that strange landscape your step
shook the earth so it cried out and split.
The unfillable chasm grew wider with warm rain,
pulling down animals, houses, trees.
You left the sinkhole unmarked, found yourself
sweating with relief, at the supermarket
choosing apples; watching TV; tapping
the calculator with a pencil. Still,
you watch sun swim through her blue glass, or,
lighting a candle you bought for her,
study the small flame until your eyes
will let in no more light. Her laugh was like water
and the books tell her name. After all you did to please her,
you fold singly into your life. You can't see
her gifts and losses in the same frame;
everything's better, and something's gone.

Nightingale

What shall I say of Henry, who patrolled
the privileged streets of Boulder with battered guitar,
loud hoarse voice and injured hands?
I'd stand mornings in his crowd until he smiled.
His eyes were unthawed blue that struck
like lightning to the gut. He built houses in the boom
until his fingers tingled and went numb.
Then he paid the rent by hitting that guitar.
He said the women who heard and stopped to listen
liked everything about him but himself.
I'm pretty sure he meant me too.
Now Boulder spits me out when I go back,
I can't climb its mountains or breathe its air.
I ask my last friend living there,
have you seen Henry, have you seen Henry,
but he hasn't, he hardly knows who Henry is.

Sleep

Striding the dewy walkway of morning, the brave
and ambitious hours, I keep it from my mind
like a drug I can't afford. Then the sirocco
of afternoon, eyes open to the blowing sand; evening
a slow seduction, the narrowing dark path.
After endless longing it denies me, withholds
until desire is bitter, an angry sweat of sheets.
I'm hooked, besotted, tortured by the way
it asks for my hand, then quibbles over my dowry.
How I earn it with righteousness, with aerobics,
with tears brought on or forced! Crowbar me
into this small space meant for dreamlessness,
for black, pure peace, unquestioned, warm.

Melancholy

What if, instead of ordering takeout for your friends,
sitting around the table for guy talk and microbrew,
while I'm out tonight you took the evening to pack
so I'd come home to find the archetypes of loss:
unshirted hangers in half the closet, empty drawers
gaping naked as new. How faithfully I trust the world
to return you to me when I return, cranky from the cold
and stamping snow from my boots.
Everything but you teaches disappointment and attrition.
Everything else moves endlessly away from heat.
Even as I imagine it, I can't imagine it: posters
stripped from the walls, computerless printer dangling cables,
the red-and-yellow tulips you gave me opened flat as hands
and spilling their black stamens on the scrubbed table.

Find the Flower

In the black-and-white photograph, find the flower
that cannot hide her colors completely, the peony
so flushed with fuchsia heat that the page
is warm to your fingertip in that spot. Mark
the location in your mind and seek her out.
Imagine the map that will get you there, the delicate
tools you will need. Memorize the particular shade
of pink so you would know it in any guise,
filtered through any stand of trees, almost
seeming to call when you have lost your way.
Train yourself to recognize the one perfume only
in a forest of scents. Imagine the questions to ask
to put you on the right path, even if there is no path,
even if the path itself is one you must imagine.

Try not to see the world as in that photo:
flat and colorless for you now unless she is in it.

Sniffing You Out

I want you rough, your redneck charm and meanness
– how a horse bites corn – not the gallantry you learned since then.
I want the tract houses and kissing cousins,
babies that come at nineteen, eighteen, seventeen,
bats that squeak by streetlights in the high Ozark night.
You make me shudder like tarpaper stapled to plywood.

Where I come from we don't call ourselves Midwestern.
Where I come from it's a mess of roots in thin soil,
yanked out for a weather change, a gold rush, a smile.
I remember the stink of green, the heat, the line
of oil wells hammering at the horizon.

I recognize your vowels, your athlete's body gone to seed,
the harvest of kids packed in your groin. I recognize
your truck-stop, pool-shark, snake-charmer past, that flight
West or East to get the shit off your shoe-sole.

You're a hot rod in a Mercedes lot. Your one leopard's spot
can't hide you from me when I smell kin.

The Climb

To get to the place I'm going, you hike
downhill a bit and cross the road
where the trucks split the air in front of you.
Then you move between light and shade,
sun and fog, as you climb the long hill,
and there's no shoulder to walk on,
and the wet grass soaks your boots. I go there
when I feel like a butterfly on a pin
of narrow want, of misdirection.
I gulp sweet air, shake soreness from my arms,
and almost always a woman is behind me
like a shadow or smaller reflection.
While I keep moving, she moves also,
but of her own volition, following
as if this is all innocence, or an illusion
not transparently doomed by the need
to drain this love of desire, or this desire
of shame. I climb, legs knotting to get me there,
and finally I see it: the whole valley lit by sun,
green farms and fields stretching into trees
and trees into morning-glory-blue horizon.
I will not turn around for her
until we are safely through this pass.

She is pushing with a hand on the wall of my back.
She is whispering, *more love, more love for us.*

Scenes I Never Made

Jack in Love

All your tough-guy humor gone goofy and slack,
this time at our monthly lunch you eat nothing,
drink two Italian beers, try hard to maintain eye contact
and ask appropriate questions. But you're

fifty-something and feeling nineteen. You've
written off death like a loser acquaintance.
You won't tell me her name, but the word "beautiful"
falls endlessly, thick as salt on bread.

You mention your business presentation
as if you're spilling flowers all over me. You reach
for the butter knife to chart this familiar terrain,
mapping it out with colored chalks, with fire-ants,

with hypodermics and lilacs and smoke.
It's a tragic loss of good conversation. Gallant as ever,
you pay with plastic, offer me your arm as we leave.
I breathe your leather-coat atmosphere,

keep from resting my cheek on your shoulder.
I know her name. I see it on your arm
and in the fog. You tilt your hat and disappear:
undercover, anachronistic, chagrined.

The Husk

When we turned off the machine
he had already left the building,

and we knew how he wanted us to act.
But we had tended the husk for five days

and we loved it more than anything
we could by then imagine. For me at least

it was a kind of heaven, this being called upon.
It was this I needed to let go, this and the hope

that persists even now: coming through the glass
double doors at the station, him standing there

waiting in his yellow jacket, small ironic smile
on his face, unable either to hide or show his pleasure.

And rushing up and grabbing him in a hug,
holding on even after he starts to back away.

Dreaming of the Dead

Overacting like a silent film star, he spat at me:
Princess-bitch, spoiled potato, garden robber,
one-way dead end, hollow pumpkin, simpering stone.

I lost my little speech of gratitude, my sweet goodbye.
All night I ran the gauntlet of excuses
to escape his eyes like cigarette tips on my skin.

Last autumn I wondered why he didn't visit me
like this, after carrying his memory through the day
lightly in my hand, robin's-egg blue and small,

after setting him to watch over us
from the mantelpiece, the bookcase, the desk.
I thought to treasure him in sleep as I forgot to

in life, when I slung him casually, daughterly,
into my pack of loved ones, folded his generosity
into the rest of my income and let the interest fatten.

Too late for his blessing, I'm paying
past dues for what might have been precious
given fewer good intentions, more grace.

Restaurant

You're dead and I'm here with your ex-wife.
Stranger things have happened, but this one
didn't occur to me before it occurred.
You so tall, so broad.
Your darkest corners now exposed,

or never to be exposed.
She was with us for every lunch:
your rage, her laziness and greed,
and once, just once I think,
how much you loved her still.

If I thought about it, I thought we'd be
here together, or out for a walk,
you steadying my arm or settling
yours on me. Loving the river,
loving the blue sky.

Instead, reeking of Chardonnay, steeped
in girlishness, I stumble back with her,
tower over her as you did.
You'd hate me for it but you're gone.
She's a lovely person.

Glimpse

Once, heading toward a different exit,
I saw him striding down the platform
and cut off my voice in my throat.

Just as, when she was still well and at home
and I had a baby for her to meet,
certain plans would have taken me there.

He worked five blocks from me;
we rode the same morning train.
I'd stop to talk to him another time.

The Nurse and the Principal

"Mr. Carpenter to the nurse's office" was the secret faculty
code for a bomb threat – an announcement
that interrupted class, and paused, and repeated,

and we hooted and whistled at this raunchy development,
the nurse and the principal going at it in the closet
with the asthma medications, alcohol swabs and blood-pressure cuff,

while our French teacher ticked over to the door
in her three-inch heels and stuck her pretty neck out,
looking left and right (these were the expert precautions:

look both ways down the hall to find the bomb) and we
were quiet in the odd static of the moment, until she turned,
snapped her fingers and started warbling transitive verbs;

but after school our English teacher told some of us
what it meant – as teachers whisper everywhere
to their favorite few – so that later, in the dark,

instead of picturing Mr. C., suitpants pooled
at his ankles, bending the nurse over her porcelain sink
to the delighted cheers of the intercom,

the mascots, pets and geeks, privileged with insider status,
fell asleep seeing purple-and-gold pennants in flames, blown
bits of brick and flesh, glass beakers just bursting to sing.

Crabs

Savino gave them to Joan who gave them to James.
Or maybe Joan gave them to Savino *and* James,

which is what I heard. I could have told James
not to go out with that slutty Joan. Wasn't I always at his elbow

when he played "Sunshine on My Shoulders"
on the practice room piano? I knew all the words,

blinking at James behind my thick glass lenses:
James of the dock siders and impeccable sweaters,

James with eyebrows like silky black caterpillars, James
the atheist bisexual, or so he said. Maybe he got them from Savino.

Maybe the three of them made a snaky, slippery heap
of limbs and genitals every Saturday afternoon while I

did homework in the library, hoping James would show up
and walk me to the bakery for a bagel, wiggling his hands in the air

like tarantulas I imagined crawling all over my skinny body.
At his New Year's Eve party I sank into the sofa,

shoulders hunched in pink angora, wanting, oh wanting
the sneery curve of his mouth, his Omar Sharif moustache,

his mathy mind, his perfect swimmer's legs
pacing off the deep pile carpet, every move a waltz.

How did I get invited to that party, anyway? I thought maybe
I had a shot, but then the crabs story surfaced: I saw Jeff

bend down to Stephanie, and she crossed the room
quickly to Kathy, who froze with a Dorito in the air,

and so on until I leaned my ear to David's mouth
and received the news like a tragic communion: crabs,

tiny Long Island lobsters washed up in the kelp, crawling the warm
salt swamp of the pubis, the petri dish of adolescent sex.

And that was it. No way would he mess with virginal me
after his first venereal disease. It was Savino

who kissed me one afternoon outside the practice room,
and I knew James wouldn't believe it, or he wouldn't care.

Jumpin' Joe

So what happened to the girl who was fucking
our fortyish math teacher, Jumpin' Joe,
who'd leap across the room to illustrate his proofs,
whom it was almost impossible to imagine
doing it with that pale majorette in the back row?

But everyone knew. I didn't even know her
and I knew. The year before, a woman slammed
into Advanced Trig and shrieked, *Who is she?*
I found the maroon glove! I can only guess
his imaginary numbers drove them wild,

and his effortless way of erasing
his latest problems with a wet sponge.
He'd show up at Honor Society functions to watch,
out of place among the parents, and say
he liked to keep up with his students. But come on.

He was all polyester and Bryl Cream and big
oily brown eyes like a seal's, and you had to wonder
where her parents thought she was every afternoon.
Where did she go, with that porcelain skin,
that unchic long red hair, that horsy smile?

Reader, she married him,
and now she lives in the hometown
where everyone knows she fucked her math teacher,
and he still teaches roomfuls of redheads,
and her tan gets deeper every year.

Virgins

It was tenderness and arrogance,
public parks and ceramic unicorns,
driving in the rain looking for a place to kiss
in his uncool mustard station wagon.

He worked nights in a popcorn factory,
brought me gigantic cans of it:
cinnamon, passion fruit, hot chili.
He fell asleep everywhere we went,

almost before I could touch him.
He said my nose was a little too small.
He despised Kahlil Gibran,
a birthday gift from me.

It was glimpsed and maddening,
Champale and Doritos,
moonlight and Tylenol,
groping on the third floor, listening for steps.

He got thrown out of my house
almost before I could touch him.
On a bench in winter he started to shake
when he gave me a garnet heart on a chain.

It was diner coffee and buttered bagels,
expressways through endless January.
We felt conspired against and noble.
He was not unwilling to cry.

It was slow dancing at pool parties.
It was transportation and pale dawn.
It was blurry pictures from a cheap camera,
red hair in his eyes, trying not to blink.

Chapter Book

1. We Move to the Country

Our Ozark farm – ten acres of weedy pasture,
squat white house, its added room sided
with tar paper, its inside sprouting wasps' nests.
Well-house, water tank I rode like a horse, horse
in the pasture with the colt who stepped on my leg
so tenderly it bruised but didn't break, bull-calf mean
and ready for killing, failed rabbits, failed goats with their kid,
green grass full of chiggers and deer ticks.
Mama washed me in Clorox when I rolled in it,
smell of laundry in the steam, acid biting into my scrapes.

Until my brother whacked the high grass down,
I wore cowboy boots up to my knees – snakes
and spiders of all poisons lived with the horseflies,
June bugs, red ants, grasshoppers, the arrowheads
and rusty tools. Everything always seeped
into where the four of us tried to be clean and quiet.
There never was a sound like that thunder, so loud
it twisted up in me, a hook, a noise like pain.
No storm cellar to run to, we stayed in the way
of any wind, any black cloud breaking up the hills.

Who knows what dusted the fields to force them
into that ecstatic green, biplane sifting something over
house and school, the animals dying suddenly
or slowly, our guts writhing with sickness no one
could ever explain. They took my mother and kept her
for weeks while the place froze me up
and even in my closet it could come to find me.
The first great good thing: Mama in her own bed,

sunning slowly like a bluebell damp with tracks,
warming where she stood till she could get us out of there.

2. I Begin My First Novel

I set out yellow pencils, scratch paper with wide-set lines.
In books they solved the mystery to great praise:
a hidden cave, diamond necklace, den of thieves.

Me, I couldn't even find my brother.
He was as not-there as he could be: bed neat,
books dusted and straight on his shelves,

every secret piece of him held in, taped down,
slicked into place. He was doing things, he was doing
something, his bedroom wouldn't tell.

So what to say? Not the dusty smell
of the general store that sold blue cream soda,
live bait and sanitary napkin belts;

not the rooster that left red marks down my legs;
not the Coleman lamp when the lights went out, or
my tiny figures from white candle-wax. Not my mother

crying in the living room late at night, my father insisting
"But there aren't any jobs for you, I looked,"
or the way she sat all day at the television,

fifteen miles from town, and no friends even there.

3. The Grownups Take Charge

When Mama's hair got too long for her, she'd pull it
into a little tail. This meant disgust for the money
burning in the woodstove and turning the curtains gray.
It meant a night of dishes and cabinets slammed

but not broken. If we could afford the hairdresser
she'd come home humming and pretty.
If she chopped it herself, it meant silence and dinner
on our own, her in the bedroom for the duration

or until the next morning when my father went to work.
He was happiest tending the horses; milking the cow
with a puppy peering from his pocket; planting potatoes
that grew small and hard as marbles; rescuing horses

from the hailstorm that gashed his forehead – the farmer
hero bloodied in battle. He was gone all day every day,
to a real-estate office in town I never saw.
I don't know if he sold a thing.

He was like a storm contained by mountains,
raging only in his four walls, peaceful out in the world
where the trees shrieked and the other men's wives
made pies every morning. And when bronchitis

choked me in the night, he wrapped me in quilts
and carried me out to breathe the cold, still air.

4. We Cut Our Losses

All of them had a chore, everyone but me, seven,
walking round and round the house in the early evening
while they weeded and hoed, dug and sprayed:

I couldn't help, could only spoil what I touched,
the carrots or the chickens, the fireflies I'd catch
and smear shining on my fingers.

Turns out they had no idea what they were doing
all those days and nights; they seemed to know,
but when Mama got sick they couldn't make up

anything else worth pretending. Too young to visit,
I waved and saw something white: her face, a pillow
held up to the hospital window. Then months

watching TV in the featureless dark – my brother
liked the light out – and eating cereal from the box.
She lived. We moved to the city and never

spoke of it: coming or going, purchase or foreclosure,
animals sold off cheap, dogs left to run wild in the hills.
We lost fair and square. We thought we could start over.

Visit

I think she asks me to come back
to see how gracelessly I can respond,
this old friend who stayed here
while I went and did whatever I've done.
Her four kids put their arms
around my neck and call me aunt.
Our history predates everything
but family; I know her from before
we decided who to be. Years of pictures
map our many hairstyles:
feathered and sprayed at fifteen,
spiked at twenty, bobbed at thirty.
In this town every rebellious cell
in me remembers scenes I never made,
having stoned sex in a pickup truck, or
splattering the pretty storefronts
with pressurized rage.
Now she nurses the youngest
while I pour juice for the rest
in her house big enough for all of them.
Her kids are calling to be held.
I'm holding them.
I'll never move back here.

Flying Dreams

I cried from joy at the movie about the Nile
in one of those dome-screen theaters where the shows
are all fifty minutes long and full of landscape
and swelling music, the other children
scattered like shells down the long row next to me.
Julia jumped in her seat, got up to leave once
and was put back. "Are we moving?" she whispered.
I told her no but I wasn't sure

since I was in my dream of flying, but wide awake
and with someone I loved, as in the pictures of Heaven
I drew during Art, with all my friends dancing on cloud floors
and climbing cloud mountains. There I was, rushing
past cliffs and over water, music everywhere
and no fear because I will only bounce
and I can do this whenever I want.

But I don't know how to have that dream,
I don't know how they make those movies,
and when it was over Julia held my hand
and we walked up the dome to blink in the light.

Laura Cherry's chapbook, *What We Planted*, was awarded the
2002 Philbrick Poetry Award by the Providence Athenaeum. She
is co-editor of the anthology *Poem, Revised* (Marion Street Press).
Her work has been published in journals including *Asphodel*,
Argestes, *Forklift: Ohio*, *H_NGM_N*, *Agenda*, *LA Review*, *Newport
Review*, *Naugatuck River River*, and *The Vocabula Review*. It has
also appeared in the anthologies *Present Tense* (Calyx Press), and
Vocabula Bound (Marion Street Press). She received an MFA from
Warren Wilson College. She lives near Boston, where she works as a
technical writer.

ISBN 098419283-2

9 780984 192830